Middle-East

Asia

Phoenicians	Sumerians	Hebrews	Chinese	Japanese	Indians	Mayas	Aztecs	Incas	First Americans

c36 000 Primitive people in Lower Yellow River Valley

30 000 B.C. people hunted.

Mexico, Andes

c50 000 — 20 000 B.C. First migrants from Asia reached North America

Phoenicians	Sumerians	Hebrews	Chinese	Japanese	Indians	Mayas	Aztecs	Incas	First Americans	Scale
										8000
										7500
										7000
										6500
										6000
										5500
										5000
		First pottery								4500
										4000
										3500
	Oldest inscribed tablet at Kish									3000
Phoenicians settle	Ur supreme									2500
		Semi-nomadic	Hsia Dynasty		Civilisation in the Indus valley					2000
Egyptian, Babylonian, Hittite influence	Hammurabi of Babylon rules	Abraham, Isaac and Jacob	Shang Dynasty		Aryans invade				Pottery in southeast of North America	1500
Phoenicians trading in Mediterranean	First Assyrian Empire	Egypt dominates	Chou Period				Culture in Mexico		Eskimo culture begins to use sea as a source of food	
Carthage established		King David					Climax of Oltec culture		'Mound Builders' inhabit Ohio Valley	1000
Persians dominate	Wars between Persians and Greeks	Israel & Judah Assyrians Babylonians	Civil wars	Yao period begins	Greeks reach India		First pryamids in Mexico			500
Greeks take Tyre		Greeks Romans take Judea	Ch'in Dynasty Han Dynasty		Greeks expelled					B.C. / A.D. (0)
Punic Wars Roman domination		Hebrew lands fall to Romans; Hebrews without homeland until 1948, when Jews given Israel	chaos and unrest		Invasions Gupta Empire					500
			China united	Classic Buddhist Japan						
			Sung Dynasty	Capital moved to Heian (Kyoto)	First Muslims rule	Maya civilisation in Yucatan	Aztec settlement on Lake islands	Machu Picchu built Inca civilisation flourishes		1000
			Yuan Dynasty Ming Dynasty		Moghul Empire					
			Ch'ing Dynasty	Civil war					White settlers cultivate Virginia	1500
			Opium Wars	Early Modern Japan			Spanish under Cortes capture Aztec lands	Spanish invasions of Inca and Maya lands	African Negroes sold as slaves	2000

Columbus reached the New World

The Ancient Britons

The Ancient Britons

Pamela Odijk

M

The Ancient Britons

Contents

The Ancient Britons: timeline

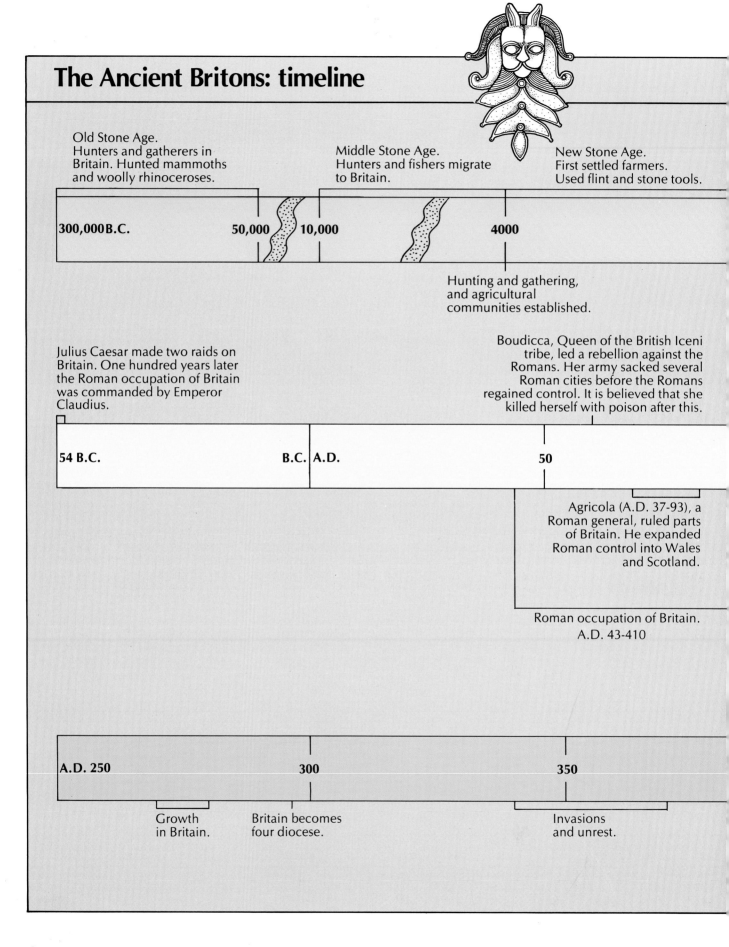

Old Stone Age.
Hunters and gatherers in
Britain. Hunted mammoths
and woolly rhinoceroses.

Middle Stone Age.
Hunters and fishers migrate
to Britain.

New Stone Age.
First settled farmers.
Used flint and stone tools.

300,000 B.C.   **50,000** | **10,000**   **4000**

Hunting and gathering,
and agricultural
communities established.

Julius Caesar made two raids on
Britain. One hundred years later
the Roman occupation of Britain
was commanded by Emperor
Claudius.

Boudicca, Queen of the British Iceni
tribe, led a rebellion against the
Romans. Her army sacked several
Roman cities before the Romans
regained control. It is believed that she
killed herself with poison after this.

54 B.C.   **B.C. A.D.**   **50**

Agricola (A.D. 37-93), a
Roman general, ruled parts
of Britain. He expanded
Roman control into Wales
and Scotland.

Roman occupation of Britain.
A.D. 43-410

A.D. 250   **300**   **350**

Growth
in Britain.

Britain becomes
four diocese.

Invasions
and unrest.

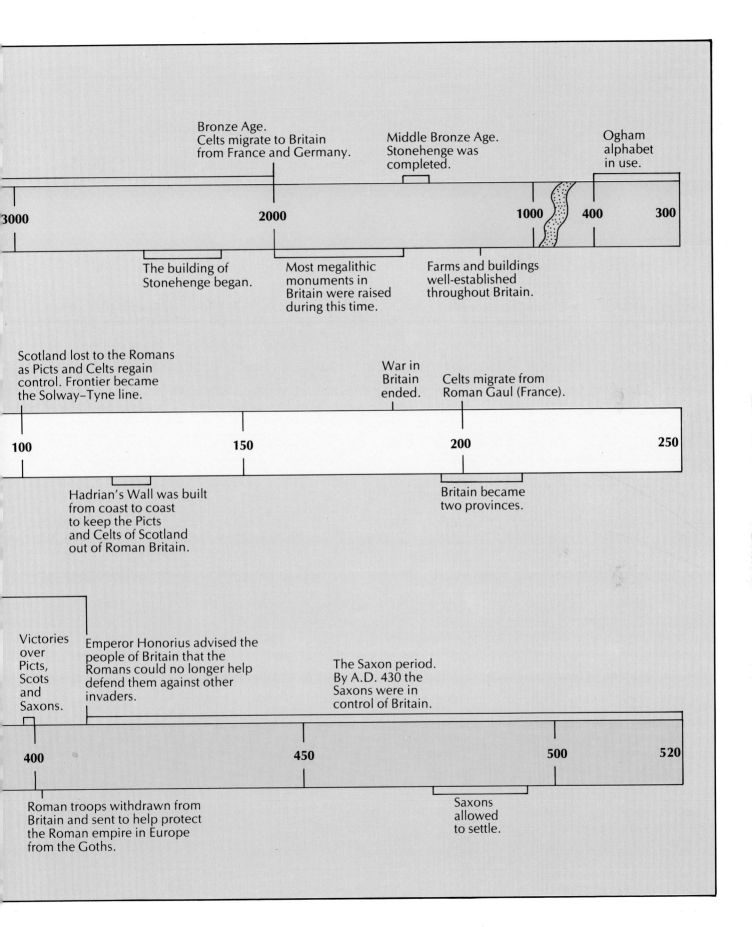

Bronze Age.
Celts migrate to Britain
from France and Germany.

Middle Bronze Age.
Stonehenge was
completed.

Ogham
alphabet
in use.

3000   **2000**   **1000**   **400**   **300**

The building of
Stonehenge began.

Most megalithic
monuments in
Britain were raised
during this time.

Farms and buildings
well-established
throughout Britain.

Scotland lost to the Romans
as Picts and Celts regain
control. Frontier became
the Solway–Tyne line.

War in
Britain
ended.

Celts migrate from
Roman Gaul (France).

100   **150**   **200**   **250**

Hadrian's Wall was built
from coast to coast
to keep the Picts
and Celts of Scotland
out of Roman Britain.

Britain became
two provinces.

Victories
over
Picts,
Scots
and
Saxons.

Emperor Honorius advised the
people of Britain that the
Romans could no longer help
defend them against other
invaders.

The Saxon period.
By A.D. 430 the
Saxons were in
control of Britain.

400   **450**   **500**   **520**

Roman troops withdrawn from
Britain and sent to help protect
the Roman empire in Europe
from the Goths.

Saxons
allowed
to settle.

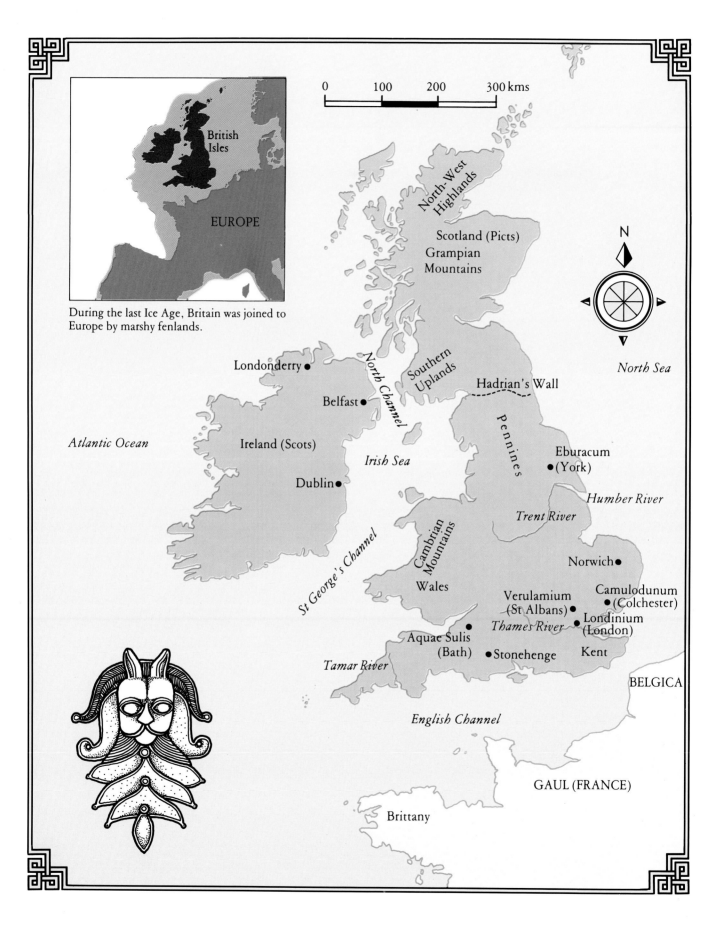

British Isles

EUROPE

During the last Ice Age, Britain was joined to Europe by marshy fenlands.

0   100   200   300 kms

N

North-West Highlands

Scotland (Picts)

Grampian Mountains

North Sea

Londonderry ●

Southern Uplands

Hadrian's Wall

Belfast ●

North Channel

Pennines

Atlantic Ocean

Ireland (Scots)

Irish Sea

Eburacum (York) ●

Humber River

Dublin ●

Trent River

Cambrian Mountains

Norwich ●

St George's Channel

Wales

Verulamium (St Albans) ●

Camulodunum (Colchester) ●

Thames River

Londinium (London) ●

Aquae Sulis (Bath) ●

● Stonehenge

Kent

Tamar River

BELGICA

English Channel

GAUL (FRANCE)

Brittany

The Ancient Britons: Introduction

The Ancient Britons were those people who, before the 5th century A.D., inhabited the area we now call the British Isles. These people fought against the Roman conquest in the 1st century A.D. unsuccessfully, and eventually adopted some Roman ways. The ancient Britons left no written records of their culture, so our knowledge of them before the Roman conquest is gained mainly from **archaeological records**.

The first people to migrate to this area did so seasonally about 300,000 years ago during the last Ice Age when the landmass of the British Isles and continental Europe was still joined. The melting ice after the Ice Age caused the seas to rise and isolated these lands and the people who had inhabited them. By 4000 B.C. these ancient Britons had become settled farmers and had learned to grow crops, raise animals, cast bronze and other metals. Between the 5th and 2nd centuries B.C. some had become traders with people on the European continent. By 200 B.C. people from Gaul (France) had settled in areas around present day Kent in south-eastern England. These people, the Celts, brought with them new knowledge and technology such as the wheeled plough. Trade contacts grew after 100 B.C.

In 55 and 54 B.C. the Romans under Julius Caesar made expeditions to Britain. Caesar assumed that the Celtic people he saw were related to the continental people. Archaeologists believe that the Celtic settlement of Britain occurred in two waves: the first wave from France and Germany in about 2000 B.C., and the second wave from Roman Gaul (France) in about 200 B.C.

Eventually the Romans, under Emperor Claudius, set out to conquer Britain. In A.D. 43, after their victory, the Romans made Britain a province of the Roman Empire called Britannia. They established towns and cities such as Camulodunum, Verulamium and Londinium (London). Our knowledge of the later Britons comes from Roman records as well as archaeological records.

When the Romans conquered Britain they found the native Britons organised into tribes. Each tribe was ruled by a king or chieftain, who had almost complete control over the tribe's territory. Some rulers shared their power with the noble class. Most of the people in each tribe were peasants. Archaeologists have, so far, identified 24 tribes of ancient Britons.

For two hundred years the Romans ruled Britain. They altered the physical appearance of the landscape by building roads, cities, and towns and also by influencing the daily lives of

Bronze statue of Boudicca, Queen of the Iceni tribe who led a revolt against the Romans in A.D. 60–61.

many Britons. By the 3rd century A.D. the Romans had divided Britain into two administrative areas, Britannia Superior with the capital at London, and Britannia Inferior with the capital at York. These were later replaced by four **diocese**.

Eventually the enemies of the Roman Empire began attacks on its frontiers which at that time stretched across northern Europe as well as the Mediterranean. The Romans withdrew their soldiers from Britain in A.D. 401 and sent them to defend their lands elsewhere.

Other people had become interested in Britannia. The Saxons had been allowed to settle, and the Picts from the north (Scotland) and the Scots (from Ireland) wanted to extend their lands. Angles, Saxons and Jutes began emigrating to Britannia from northern Europe. The ancient Britons entered a period of upheaval beginning in the 5th century and by A.D. 520 the Saxons were in control of Britain and the culture of the ancient Britons was again altered.

The civilisation of the ancient Britons has long disappeared and while their contribution to world civilisation might have been overshadowed by stronger and more enduring cultures, it should not be forgotten or discounted.

The Ancient Britons: Some Important Events

300,000– (50,000 years ago)	Old Stone Age The first people migrated from Europe to Britain via the landbridge that joined these areas. These first people were nomadic hunters and gatherers, who occupied the British Isles during the warmer periods.
10,000– (4000 B.C.)	Middle Stone Age The earth's climate became warmer, causing the sea-levels to rise. The landbridge the people had crossed from Europe to Britain gradually went underwater. The warmer climate brought changes to animal and plant life. New groups of people migrated from Europe. They were hunters and fishers. They hunted and trapped small animals and birds using bows and arrows with flint arrowheads.
4000– (2000 B.C.)	New Stone Age The Celts from France and Germany emigrated to Britain. These people were the first settled farmers. They cultivated the land and established farms in the uplands and downlands where the soils were light and easy to farm. They used flint and stone tools, and introduced the first plough.
2000– (700 B.C.)	Bronze Age People migrating from Europe to Britain brought with them knowledge of various metals, such as tin, copper and gold. When melted tin and copper are mixed, bronze is made. Bronze was used to make tools and ornaments. Everyday objects were made from pottery.
700 B.C.– (A.D. 43)	The Iron Age During this period, Celts from Roman Gaul (France) migrated to Britain. They brought with them a new metal, iron, which they used to make beautiful ornaments and tools, including the plough. With new and stronger tools, they cleared heavily wooded valleys and settled there. These Celts settled in south-eastern Britain, around Kent.
A.D. 43–410	Roman Britain.
A.D. 60–61	Revolt led by Boudicca, Queen of the Iceni.

The Importance of Landforms and Climate

Up until about 10,000 B.C., at the start of the Middle Stone Age, Britain was joined to the landmass of Europe, and people were able to travel there from Europe by land. When the earth's climate began to warm up, the **polar ice cap** around the North Pole began to melt, causing the seas to rise. The landbridge that had joined Britain and Europe was covered by water making Britain a separate and isolated group of islands. Because of this isolation, the people who had inhabited Britain developed a different culture from their cousins on mainland Europe.

The landforms of Britain influenced settlement. When the first settled farmers migrated to Britain about 6,000 years ago, they settled in the downland and uplands where the soils were lighter, rather than in the heavily forested valley areas where the soils were heavier. The first settlers didn't have a plough, and they used stone and flint tools, unsuitable for cultivating heavy soils.

During the Iron Age, the Celts moved into the heavily forested valleys of south-eastern England, cleared the land and established farming settlements. They used an iron-tipped plough.

In Britain over time, there have been fluctuations in the levels of the sea and this has had an effect on the coastline and the pattern of rivers further inland which eventually make their way to the sea. The sea was higher before the 1st century A.D. and in the 3rd century A.D. very wet conditions caused many parts of Britain (and Europe) to flood, causing problems in the lowland areas and harbours.

Cattle were introduced to the British Isles by the first farmers who settled there in about 4000 B.C.

Animals such as pigs sought shelter in the English woodlands, which were the last areas to be settled by the ancient Britons.

Climate

The climate of Britain in Roman times was similar to that of present day Britain, so vegetation and animal life have altered very little over the last 2,000 years.

Britain's climate is affected by the seas that surround the island. Winters are mild and summers are cool. Rainfall is highest in the northern areas. Snow falls during the winter months but stays on the ground for no longer than a few days, except in the hilly areas. Fogs are common in Britain. Frosts also occur, but less frequently in coastal areas. In the times of the ancient Britons, crops were grown along the coastal areas because of the longer growing season.

Britain's climate also experiences a high humidity. The ancient Britons had corn drying kilns in which to dry the unripe corn harvest to protect it from being damaged by the damp.

Even in an area as small as Britain, the differences in landforms and climate from place to place determine to a large extent the type of farming activities people can indulge in, and hence the type of life they can lead.

Low rainfall in places made the ground too dry for grassland and heavy soils in some areas made farmwork more difficult. As a result cattle were confined to certain areas, (usually the south-west), with dairy production being carried out on the lowlands where shelter and grass were readily available. Other cattle which could adapt more easily were kept on higher areas. Sheep which were more mobile and able to survive in colder conditions were found in the uplands. Pigs, who needed less grassland but sought shelter were better suited to the woodlands.

Natural Plants, Animals and Birds

The warming of the earth's climate during the end of the last Ice Age in about 10,000 B.C. affected the vegetation of Britain, and the kinds of animals which the new vegetation could support. The ancient **tundra** vegetation of colder times changed and forests began to grow. These forests covered most of the land which had heavy clay soils. The new forests provided homes for badgers, otters, foxes, stoats, weasels, squirrels, mice, hedgehogs, rabbits and hares. Instead of the reindeer who once inhabited this area, red deer and elk now made their homes there.

By about 4000 B.C. the climate enabled people to grow crops as well as hunt wild animals. They learned to **domesticate** certain animals, and the domesticated pigs found both forage and shelter in the oak forests.

Although new forests began to grow in Britain at the end of the last Ice Age, there was not the great variety of vegetation as the rising seas separated Britain from the landmass of Europe and many species did not reach there. Although there may not have been the variety of plants and trees as in Europe, the vegetation did range from thick forests to grasslands and marshlands, all of which the ancient Britons learned to use.

Bird life was plentiful. As well as supporting many native species of birds, Britain is also in the path of migrating birds. The seas surrounding Britain supplied an abundant variety of fish and shellfish, as well as seals, dolphins and whales.

The brown bear was one of the animals that found a home in the dense forests and open woodlands that grew in England at the end of the last Ice Age.

Crops, Herds and Hunting

The first people to inhabit Britain were hunters and gatherers, who moved around in search of food. When they migrated to Britain during the Old Stone Age (300,000−50,000 years ago), the climate, and animal and plant life were very different to that found by the Romans in the 1st century A.D. During the coldest part of the year, Britain was uninhabitable and these hunters and gatherers moved south. During the warmer part of the year, trees and plants grew, and the hunters and gatherers hunted animals such as mammoths, woolly rhinoceros, giant deers and reindeers.

During the New Stone Age (4000−2000 B.C.) the ancient Britons had established farms to grow crops, and continued to hunt and gather food. Flint was used to make tools. Hard **volcanic rock** was used to make axe blades. Timber was cut from the forests for building materials and fuel.

By 1200 B.C. the ancient Britons had established farms in the more fertile lands toward the south. Various kinds of grain were grown including barley, **emmer**, corn, rye and oats as well as vegetables and **hemp**. Flax, used to make textiles, was also grown for its oil bearing seeds.

The Celtic farmers who migrated to Britain during the Iron Age introduced crops such as the Celtic bean and a type of wheat called spelt as well as tools such as the iron-tipped plough. The Celts established small farms and settlements.

Celtic farms seem to have been stable, orderly communities and organised for communal tasks. Farms in the lowlands were often protected by embankments or dykes enclosing both pastures and arable land so herds could be brought into safe areas. It is thought these dykes were built between A.D. 10 to 20.

Harvesting

The exact methods of reaping and storing grain are not known but it is quite probable that corn was cut with a bill hook or reaping hook and dried in special ovens or kilns if it was too damp to be stored. Ears of corn would have been threshed before storage. Wild grains and weeds were often harvested along with other grain crops. After the harvest, animals would be turned out onto the fields to graze the stubble. Their manure was used to fertilise the fields.

Grain was stored in pits below the ground which were lined with dry stones to prevent the growth of mould. Grain was also stored in timber granaries above ground. The above ground granaries were square or rectangular buildings, built on stilts to protect the grain from rats and mice, and to allow air circulation.

Flint spearhead from the New Stone Age, 4000–2000 B.C.

Herds

In some regions, particularly in the uplands and the lands to the north, raising cattle was more important than growing crops although farms needed cattle and sheep to manure the fields. Herd manure was necessary because without it grain production could not be maintained. Pigs were also raised where nearby oak forests provided forage and shelter. Sheep and goats were also raised. Horses were known and used in ancient Britain, most probably in warfare and transport, rather than farming.

Cattle and sheep were reared in large numbers while pigs were of minor importance. Dogs were also kept as pets and work animals.

Julius Caesar, after his visits to Britain in 55 and 54 B.C., described the numerous farms and large numbers of cattle owned by the Britons.

Roman Influence

When the Romans arrived in Britain they found an efficient agricultural system which was similar to their own. However, the Romans brought with them and introduced to the ancient Britons new farming techniques, new crops and new tools such as scythes, the **coulter** and the vallus.

With the Roman conquest of Britain, the large numbers of soldiers stationed there had to be fed so larger areas of land were given over to growing cereal crops, often where none had been grown previously. In many places the old Celtic farms were replaced by large Roman estates with villas. The Romans established their farms on the richest soils, leaving the poorer soils for the small peasant farmers.

Reconstruction of an Iron Age farm, in Hampshire, south-east England.

How Families Lived

The ancient Britons were organised into tribes, and ruled by either a chieftain or a king, who had complete control over a tribe's territory. Some rulers shared control with the noble class, who were often called upon to advise the ruler. Most ancient Britons, however, were peasants. Each farmer usually only had enough land to support his family and pay taxes.

Iron Age farmers, like Bronze Age farmers, were crop growers and kept herds of cattle and flocks of sheep. Men hunted red deer, wild pigs and beavers, and cranes. Women made pots, spun yarn and wove cloth on upright looms.

Celtic family life was centred on the home and farming. Most items needed were produced as homecrafts.

Woollen fabrics were made from wool, which was cleaned using bone and antler combs, spun with a hand-spindle and woven. Yarn was dyed using vegetable dyes such as **woad**.

Basket making and matting were also carried out especially where pottery was scarce. Rushes were used for basket weaving.

Leather work involved skinning and tanning. The making of leather articles was another useful and necessary craft. Harnesses and clothing were the main items made from leather.

Ironwork such as tools and weapons were also made within communities. Smelting and forging took place at each homestead and small furnaces have been found at Kesor in Devon. Broken implements were often reforged. By the 5th century iron had replaced bronze as the main metal. Bronze continued to be used for the manufacture of vessels, trinkets and horse trappings.

Houses

When the Romans conquered Britain in the 1st century A.D. the Briton peasants lived in houses made of wood and clay, with thatched roofs. In the middle of the house, a fire was kept lit at most times, and smoke escaped through a hole in the roof. These round wooden huts were first built in Britain by the Celts who migrated there in about 2000 B.C. Temporary shelters were used by the nomadic herdsmen. Earlier houses were built of wood and have not survived. Some remains of Middle Stone Age houses made from stone have been found on the Orkney Islands.

Furniture was scarce in pre-Roman houses. The Romans wrote that the people sat on the ground or floor to eat, and slept on the ground upon animal skins. Tables were raised platforms slightly above the level of the ground. In later times simple bench type furniture was used. Chests were used to store things but people had few possessions beyond household utensils and tools.

Roman bath, built in the 1st century A.D. at Aquae Sulis (Bath).

Influence of the Romans

Roman villas were built in the towns and even wealthier Britons built Roman style villas in the country areas. Many of these had hot air systems (called hypocaust), glazed windows and tessellated floors and baths. In the towns the houses had running water and sewerage systems. Walls were painted and decorated, and furniture was similar to that used in ancient Rome.

Under Roman occupation, potteries, furniture manufacturers, schools of trades people and artists were established to provide equipment and decorations for Roman houses. Weaving mills were set up to produce cloth and uniforms for the Roman army.

Education

Celtic education was confined to the scholarly or priestly **Druids**. Education was by memory,

Interior of a reconstructed Iron Age farmhouse. In the middle of the house is the hearth, used for cooking and warmth. The inset shows the outside of the house. The frame is constructed from tree trunks and covered with a thatched roof. The walls are made of mud and wattle.

question and response as there were no written lessons. The Romans, on the other hand, brought with them their own system of education, and made arrangements for children of leading Britons to be educated in Latin. To be able to participate in commercial life it was necessary to know enough Latin words and numbers to be able to record a transaction.

However, in spite of the Roman presence, life in the more remote parts of Britain altered little. Life in the towns was more under Roman influence.

Food and Medicine

Posidonius, the Greek philosopher (circa 135 to 51 B.C.), described Celtic meals as consisting generally of meat (which was either boiled or roasted) and beer. However, porridge, bread and milk products including milk, butter, cheese and curds, were also part of the diet. Beef and pork were favourite meats, and the ready supply of salt (especially at salt works such as the one at Dorset) enabled animals killed in the autumn to be preserved for the winter.

Cauldrons suspended by long chains over a fire were used to cook meats and vegetables. The wealthier class drank wine but most people were fond of mead or an ale called corma.

Malt from barley, wheat, rye and oats was used to make alcoholic drinks which were fermented in vats. Breads of various kinds were also made from ground grains.

Larger portions of meat served at meals were called the "hero's portion" and were awarded to the finest warrior present as a ritual honour. Often contests were fought for this honour. Among the Celtic upper class, at least, food and drink seemed to have been in good supply.

Eggs, wild duck, geese, game and fish supplemented the diet. Seaweed was eaten in some parts, particularly Ireland. This was probably carrageen which was boiled with milk and strained. Although food was generally cut with a knife, it was eaten with the fingers.

Celtic bronze jugs inlaid with coral and enamel, from the 4th century B.C.

Above: detail from the Aylesford bucket which was used at banquets for diluting wine with water. The bucket, made from wood with metal fittings, was excavated at a 1st century B.C. grave at Aylesford in Kent.

Entertainment

Entertainment was part of feasting. At times this was noisy and rowdy, and involved mock battles or combats. Also **bards** would entertain those assembled, accompanying themselves on a musical instrument resembling a lyre.

The Roman Influence

The Romans continued to eat in the same way as they had done in Rome. The Romans not only introduced new foods to some of the ancient Britons but brought with them Roman eating habits.

Some higher class Britons, who most frequently came into contact with the Romans, adopted some Roman eating habits which included attending dinner parties which were held in traditional Roman style with people reclining to eat.

Medicine

The Romans understood little about Celtic medicine. In Celtic society mistletoe was regarded as being very important, especially to the Druids, who were the learned and medical class. The word for mistletoe in Irish and Scottish Gaelic is *uil-ioc*, which has the meaning "all healing". Weeds and herbs as well as some metals such as copper and zinc first appeared in the Bronze Age as having traditional uses in medicines. However, we know very little about Celtic medical practice.

The Celts from the earliest times developed a medical service. The legendary ruler (from Irish mythology) Macha Mong Ruadh boasted of founding a hospital in 300 B.C. The Celts ensured care for the sick which included providing nourishing food and curative care and treatment, this being the responsibility of the whole tribe. The qualifications for Celtic physicians was controlled by law.

Roman Medicine

The Roman troops were accompanied by a medical corps and on sculptures and other decorations wounded legionaries are shown being taken to dressing stations or being bandaged. There were also hospitals for sick soldiers. Descriptions of poultices, dressings and plasters have been found including some made from unusual substances such as spiders' webs soaked in oil and vinegar.

Below: Stone Age pot excavated at Windmill Hill, Avebury which is about 32 kilometres (20 miles) north of Stonehenge.

Clothes

During the New Stone Age Britons wore clothes made from animal skins. Spinning and weaving cloth, carried out in Europe, was not yet known in Britain. Skins were sewn together with bone needles. Some clothes were fastened together with bone pins. Bone and ivory necklaces from this period have been found at excavations, and these give us an idea of the jewellery worn by the ancient Britons.

By the Bronze Age, the Britons had learnt how to spin and weave cloth. The Celts wore simple clothing of coarse linen and wool which were either undyed or brightly dyed with blue obtained from woad, red from shellfish, and purple made by combining red and blue.

Men wore trousers with a tunic or shirt usually belted at the waist. A cloak was worn over this, and the length of the cloak indicated the status of the wearer. Cloaks were fastened with brooches.

Women wore a long single garment made of flax or wool, and a cloak fastened with a brooch, too.

Leather shoes and sandals were worn by men and women and sometimes linen shoes with soles made of leather were worn.

Celtic clothing generally was colourful and lavish with the Celts showing a passion for personal ornaments. Prehistoric jewellery found in graves has ranged from decorative goldwork to jet and stone necklaces.

The Britons shaved their cheeks but allowed a moustache to grow, and Strabo the Greek geographer (63 B.C. to A.D. 21), noted that most Celts were blonde and this was maintained by washing their hair constantly in lime water. Caesar remarked that the Britons he saw were clean shaven although they allowed their hair to grow long, and dressed themselves in animal skins.

The Briton queen, Boudicca, was described as having masses of red hair which fell to her knees, and as wearing a gold necklet made up of ornate pieces, a multi-coloured robe and a thick cloak held together by a brooch.

1st century A.D. enamelled bronze armband, found in North Britain.

Opposite: clothes worn by the Celts in about the 4th century B.C.

Roman Influences

Roman dress became quite popular in Britain from the 1st century onwards and many Britons began wearing the **toga**. Women wore the Roman **stola** with an under-garment called a **subucula**. White was the popular colour but poorer people wore unbleached garments.

Romans greatly admired the Celtic cloaks, especially the *Birrus Britannicus*, a heavy woollen cloak with a hood which was the best quality known in the Roman world.

During Roman times there were many hairdressers' and barbers' shops as Romans were clean shaven. (Bronze and iron shaving implements were used.) Roman women, with time to spend on personal adornment, wore quite elaborate hairstyles.

Above: solid gold Celtic torques, which were worn around the neck.

Religion and Rituals of the Ancient Britons

Religious belief in ancient Britain was influenced by the Celtic cults already present in Britain before the arrival of the Romans; the cults of the official Roman religion; and the cults brought to Britain from other places by traders and soldiers. Christianity became important in later times.

The Celtic Religion

Religion and superstition played an important role in the everyday life of the Celts. Gods were ever-present and ever-menacing and had to be placated. The gods could also be generous and helpful. Places of worship included springs, bogs, rivers, rocks and very old trees and groves of trees. Little is known about the Celtic religion because the secrets were strictly guarded. All traditional lore, history and ritual was entrusted to the Druids who were the Celtic learned and priestly class. The Druids mediated between people and their gods. The Celtic gods were usually ancient heroes or heroines, and the ancestors of the people, rather than spirit creator gods.

Bronze head from the 1st century A.D. thought to be the Celtic goddess Brigit.

The Severed Head

The Celts believed that the human head was the seat of the soul and the essence of being. It was also believed that the head remained alive after the death of the body and that the head could avoid evil, as well as prophesise and preside over the Otherworld feast. Hundreds of heads were fashioned from stone by the Celts, and warriors beheaded their foes in battle. Human heads have been found in Celtic hill forts where some were suspended from gateways or put on posts around the ramparts.

The Celts also believed in the magical power of the number three. Some mythological characters had three heads. The Druids, in the form of triads, taught sentences of three phrases.

The Druids

The Celtic religion was presided over by the Druids, the learned and priestly class. One interpretation of the word Druid is "knowing (or finding) the oak tree", and the Druids seem to have had a close association with oak trees and oak forests. To become a Druid, one was required to undergo twenty years of training.

The Druids took charge of public and private sacrifices and were the teachers. They also mediated between the people and their gods. Female Druids (or Druidesses) also played a part in Celtic religion and are mentioned by Roman writers.

The Druids were suppressed by the Romans and the later Christians, and they became the poets, historians and judges instead of the priests. The Romans also offered the sons of the Briton nobility an education in Latin as an alternative to the education offered by the Druids.

Part of a plaque found at Gwynned in Wales, from the 1st century A.D. The motif is believed to represent a major Celtic divinity.

Some Celtic Gods and Goddesses

Lug (or Lugh)	King of the gods.
Manannán	God of the sea.
Nuada of the Silver Arm (or Nuadu)	God sometimes associated with Fishermen and the sea.
Dagda	"The Good God".
The three gods of Danann	Lug received his weapons from these three gods.
Ogma	Irish god of eloquence equivalent to the Gaulish god Ogmios.
Brigit (of which there were three)	Brigid, goddess of poetry; Brigit, goddess of healing; and, Brigit, goddess of smithcraft. Also known as Brigantia.
Morrígan Badb Nemain	Goddesses of battle.
Taranis	A warrior god.
Corinivm	An antlered god.
Cernunnos	A horned god linked with fertility, sometimes called the "lord of the animals".
Epona	Goddess of horses and a mother goddess.
Genii Cuccullati	Represented as three mysterious hooded figures.

23

Roman Gods

In later times the gods of Rome, particularly Jupiter, Juno and Minerva, and the Roman emperor himself, were worshipped. Traders and soldiers who were influenced by religions that they had seen in other cultures also introduced these to the ancient Britons. In some places, Celtic and Roman gods were combined and worshipped. There was also a shared belief in spirits, ancestor spirits and ghosts, as well as in curses and spells. Tablets with curses written backwards have been found throughout Britain.

Christianity

Christianity was beginning to influence people in Britain by the 5th century A.D. Christianity did not have a strong influence in Britain before the 4th century A.D., even though there were some Christian **martyrs** during the 3rd century A.D.

Celtic grave in Ireland. The stone tomb is hidden under piles of rock.

Burial Customs

In the New Stone Age, the people of ancient Britain buried their dead in communal graves. There were two main types of communal graves: the first were stone tombs which were hidden under piles of rocks, and the other type were long barrows or mounds of earth under which timber structures were built.

The Celts who were in Britain by 200 B.C. **cremated** their dead. The Romans also cremated their dead until the 2nd century A.D.

At excavated burial sites, funerary carts have been discovered, and yet in other places careful burial procedures were not always followed, and the bodies were disposed of with little ceremony. Cremation became common from the 1st century B.C. The ashes of the deceased were buried in urns within a defined cemetery area.

Obeying the Law

Celtic Britain and Celtic Law

Early Britons were under the control of several kings and kingdoms all of which had different laws. This made the system of Celtic law very complex. However, Irish and Welsh laws do tell us something about ancient Celtic traditions and how the society was controlled. The

This bronze figure, from the Roman-Britain period, is thought to represent a Druid. Under Roman occupation, the Druids were persecuted because the Romans feared their influence. Many Druids went into hiding.

law tracts in written form go back to the 7th century A.D., but the laws themselves probably date back to the Iron Age and the language in which the laws were written was deliberately obscure. The law system of Ireland was known as the **Brehon Laws** with the judge being called *breitheamh*.

The *filid*, who were prophets or seers, were the traditional custodians of the law and these people may have been equally respected with the Druids.

Much of the law was passed on orally in verse (to make memorising it easier) and the law was regarded as a science and the secrets were carefully guarded.

The laws were very complex and involved a long list of observances and taboos. There were laws for all social situations. Compensation for wrongs suffered by a person was made according to the social rank of the person, and depended on the extent of damage suffered. This was called an honour price or *lóg-n-enech*. There were no prisons. Lawbreakers lost their civil rights within a community until they had satisfied the fines or obligations imposed upon them.

One of the most unusual elements of the law was the use of fasting, often in front of the accused's house from sunrise to sunset to force that person to fast also and to seek arbitration. Should the person ignore the fast and not pay, that person's honour was lost.

Great emphasis was placed on fairness, appropriateness, and the power of truth, as well as taking care of the poor, sick and aged.

Divorce was permitted and was reasonably easy to obtain. There was also the custom of marriage for one year, after which both parties could dissolve the marriage. There were ten types of marriage listed in ancient Irish law.

Roman Law and the Britons

After the Romans conquered Britain, many of the kings retained their titles but, instead of being independent, they obeyed the directions and laws laid down by their Roman conquerors. The Romans reorganised the kingdoms as local government unites, called *civitates*.

Roman Law

The Romans forbade civilians to carry weapons, and the Britons were required to pay tribute to Rome and the Romans. Roman society was divided into two groups, an upper division (*honestiores*) who included the soldiers and the lower division (*humiliores*). The Romans also instituted a system of taxation. There were two types of taxation:

Tribulum soli which was a tax on land and fixed property. The conquered lands were considered Roman and those who occupied the land were required to pay rent. Taxes were paid in coins but occasionally grain and hides were accepted. These taxes and supplies went toward paying for the Roman armies and officials.
Tribulum capitis which was a tax on all other property, manufactured and traded. There were additional taxes in the form of customs duties.

Non-Romans who became Romans were subjected to these taxes.

Roman law was enforced in Roman courts and applied to Roman citizens. A Roman who married a non-citizen could make arrangements to have the marriage recognised by Roman law so the children of the marriage could inherit property. However, the wife was not regarded as a Roman citizen.

The right to Roman citizenship was given automatically at the end of military service into which many Britons were recruited. Citizenship was sometimes granted for special services such as the holding of government or official office. Free people who were not given Roman citizenship were called *peregrini*. The *peregrini* conducted their own affairs according to their own laws.

Slavery existed in Britain in pre-Roman times but it was more entrenched in Roman society.

Writing it Down: Recording Things

The languages spoken in pre-Roman Britain are referred to as Breton and insular Celtic languages. Insular Celtic was different from the Celtic language spoken on the European mainland. The insular language was further divided into two groups called Irish (Goidelic or Gaelic) and British (often called Brythonic), but scholars are still learning about the use of language in ancient Britain. In the 15th century, mystery plays and religious works in Breton were recorded. It has been suggested that the Celts took their name from *ceilt* (to *conceal*), and that they were called "the hidden people" because they were reluctant to commit their knowledge to writing.

Ogham Alphabet

The **ogham alphabet** dating from the 4th century A.D., was the alphabet used by the Celtic population of the British Isles.

The alphabet consists of 20 letters which are divided into four groups (*aicme*), each containing five letters. The ogham alphabet is similar to the Scandinavian runes.

After the Romans arrived in Britain there were two spoken languages: Celtic, and Latin which was the Roman language. Most people in the countryside spoke Celtic while Latin became the language of the towns where the upper classes lived. Many people spoke both languages.

Early written records from ancient Britain and Roman times include inscriptions on stone, trade marks on manufactured goods, letters and documents, and **graffiti**. Roman coins are records from which information can be gained by studying the images on the coins which were important symbols of the time.

The Romans, who brought with them a de-veloped writting language from Rome, wrote on parchment or vellum with ink using a reed pen or an iron stylus.

Reading

Before the Romans arrived in Britain, the Britons could not read and write as all information was passed on orally. Even in Roman times reading was a skill usually confined to the townspeople and the upper classes. People of the countryside generally could not read the written word.

The Ogham Stone with Ogham characters inscribed on it. Most of the inscriptions found are names.

Calendar

The calendar of the ancient Celts was a religious one. The year was divided into two periods beginning with the feast of *Beltaine* (1 May), the summer festival, and *Samain* (1 November) thought to mean "end of summer". Each of these periods was then equally divided by the feasts of *Imbolc* (1 February) thought to be a purification feast for farmers, and *Lughnasa* (1 August). All feasts and seasons had special rituals which were performed by the Druids.

Druids were much concerned with calendrical computations. Fragments of the remarkable **Coligny Calendar**, a huge bronze plate with a calendar of 62 consecutive lunar months has been found. The language is in Gaulish but it reckons in nights in true Celtic fashion and marks lucky and unlucky days.

Stonehenge in South England was started in the 3rd millennium B.C. and completed in the Middle Bronze Age.

Stonehenge

Stonehenge is a huge structure which was built at Wiltshire in about 2000 B.C., with additions being made years later. The stones which are arranged in circles and archways enabled observations to be made of the sun, moon and eclipses. It also enabled 29 day and 20 day lunar months to be counted. Other structures similar to Stonehenge have been found in Britain, and it is assumed that they were used to study the stars and heavens, and as a calendar.

Weights and Measures

The Britons adopted the Roman system of weights and measures, with the Roman measure of weight *Libra* eventually being written as the British pound (lb.).

The Roman mile remained a measure of distance in Britain. It was not until the Middle Ages that the current English system of weights and measures came into use.

Legends and Literature of the Ancient Britons

Very little is known about the Celtic literature and nothing survives of the original legends of the ancient Britons. Before Roman times, knowledge was in the hands of the Druids, whose duties included knowing the sagas, geneaologies and histories of their people, and composing appropriate poems. It was also their duty to record new knowledge.

Some early verses of the Celtic oral tradition, were later preserved in passages of written documents.

Ordinary people are seldom mentioned in the ballads and sagas, which deal mainly with kings, nobles and warrior heros. Women played an important part in the Irish sagas, though they were always portrayed as ladies, and not women of the common people.

Tales of the Stones

There is a variety of folktales and legends about the standing stones and megaliths of which Stonehenge is an example. Although these legends were written down in later times, it is quite possible that they had their origins in the time of the ancient Britons. Some of these legends are common to all areas. In many legends people were supposed to have been turned to stone and, in others, there is the belief that these stones are unable to be counted unless certain rituals were performed. Other legends claim that the stones came to life at certain times and went to nearby streams to wash and drink. There are also legends about the healing properties of the stones.

Glastonbury Tor, an ancient Briton earth-work, associated with early Briton legends and mysteries.

Birds and Animals in Celtic Mythology

Bronze statuettes of boars, from the 1st century B.C. The boar features in much Celtic mythology.

Birdlore and bird superstitions are popular in Celtic mythology. Perhaps this has its foundations in the Druids who drew omens from bird flights and bird calls, and who believed that the water birds were once associated with the healing power of the sun. The sun was often depicted as a cormorant and there were statues of chariots being drawn by birds. Ducks occur frequently in Celtic mythology as do cranes, owls and swans, with cranes being depicted as sinister.

Animals, too, had their place in mythology, especially the boar which was a favourite animal of the ancient Britons. Other animals mentioned include the stag, horse, bull, ram and dog.

Of all water creatures, the salmon was most featured in stories. The salmon was supposed to have eaten the nuts from the sacred hazeltree as they fell into a pool which renewed the salmon's wisdom and supernatural powers.

Legends of Lug, King of the Gods

Lug of the Long Arm possessed a magic spear that roared and flashed fire. Lug used this spear in the battle of Moytura to liberate King Nuada (Nuadu) from the Fomori, the one eyed deamons of the night. Nuada then entrusted Lug with the defence of Ireland. Those who came to help before the battle were Goibniu, who could make any weapon; Dianceht, the physician who made a Silver Arm for Nuada, and who could cure all wounds; Credne, the brazier who made rivets for spears, hilts for swords, and bosses and rims for shields; and Dagda, who had a magic club, a cauldron of plenty which none could leave without being fully satisfied, and a harp which could play three tunes—a lullaby, sadness and happiness, all at once. In battle Lug knocks out the evil eye of the king of the Fomori with a stone from his sling and this eye devours all the other Fomori.

Pangur the Cat

The earliest surviving poem written in Irish was one written in about A.D. 800 by a scribe from Kildare. It was a poem of eight stanzas in which the poet compares his actions with those of his white cat called Pangur. The poem begins with:

> "... I and Pangur Ban my cat
> 'Tis a like task we are at;
> Hunting mice is his delight
> Hunting words I sit all night..."

Art and Architecture

The Celts who came to Britain during the Iron Age were skilled craftsmen who fashioned beautiful jewellery and ornaments from bronze, gold, iron and precious stones. Celtic art developed in Britain from the 3rd century B.C., and reached its peak in the first century A.D. Iron and bronze were used in the manufacture of decorative articles. Asymmetric patterns in which nothing is as it first appears was a Celtic characteristic. It concentrated on animals and birds as subjects with faces often being inset with eyes of red glass. Most art objects were for ceremonial use and included drinking horn mounts, helmets and shields.

After Roman times objects such as brooches, belt buckles and hanging bowls appeared in Britain. They were Roman in design but had Celtic patterns.

In Ireland, which escaped the direct impact of the Romans, art had a continuity, where the pagan element and the anti-Christian element were obvious.

Stone Sculpture

Many stone idols which were pagan objects of worship were smashed by the Christians, and others were adapted by them. One of the best known and most fascinating objects is the Turoe Stone, a granite boulder trimmed in a dome-like shape and covered with decorative motifs. It is thought to date from the 3rd century B.C.

As the Celts worshipped certain stones and believed them to be under direct control of the gods, the Turoe Stone was probably one of these. Other similar stones have been found in Ireland. Many stone figures have been found which probably had replicas in wood but which have since been destroyed. Stone figures of animals, birds and heads have been found, all of which had a place in Celtic beliefs.

Ancient Carvings

All over Britain dozens of rock faces, including rock tombs, have been discovered which have abstract and ornamental carvings. They all have a broadly similar pattern of **cup-and-ring marks**, spirals and **concentric circles**. The meaning of these markings is still not properly understood.

The Turoe Stone in Galway, Ireland, was carved in the 1st century A.D.

Above: bronze shield decorated with studs in red glass paste. The shield, from the 1st century B.C., was found in the Thames River.

Celtic Mirrors

Celtic mirrors, confined to southern Britain, were made of bronze. They were made in Britain from the late 1st century B.C. onwards, and show fine artistic skill. Possession of these was a mark of wealth and status. Mirror designs were based on three circles linked together. The handles were works of art being wrought in elegant bronze shapes.

Other Metalwork

By the 2nd century B.C. local craftsmen were producing quite accomplished works of art. Some of the most impressive of early British pieces found by archaeologists include a scabbard of a daggar found in the Wisbeck area of Cambs, and a shield found in the Witham River in 1826, together with a mounting from a scabbard and a pony cap. Many of these objects were made for parade purposes. Again, metalwork articles had the characteristic Celtic symmetrical design.

Enamelling

Horse bits and harnesses were often enamelled with red being the most popular colour, as it was the colour associated with battle. Enamelling was widely practiced in the eastern and northern areas of Britain. Sometimes blue glass was combined with the enamel.

Below: Celtic bronze mirror from Aston in Hertfordshire. Celtic mirrors were highly polished to make them reflective.

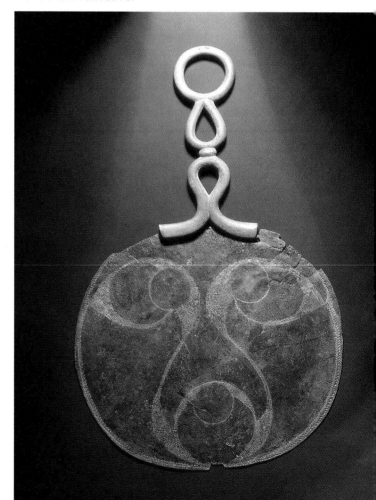

Pottery

A considerable amount of pottery was produced in Britain and each had a well-defined regional style such as the scratched cordoned bowls of Wessex made in very fine black, fired red, and then scratched in geometric patterns. Very little is known about the early pottery production centres.

Architecture

Stonehenge

Stonehenge is the best known and most outstanding surviving structure of ancient Britain. It was built in about 2000 B.C. and added to over the centuries. It consists of circles of large standing stones and earthworks. Some of the stones in the structure are up to 9 metres (30 feet) long and weigh up to 51 tonnes (50 tons). Scholars have not found evidence indicating that Stonehenge was used by the Druids for any other purpose than observing the heavens, eclipses and to calculate and count the lunar months. Other structures similar to Stonehenge are scattered throughout Britain.

The Roman Influence

The Romans built towns throughout Britain and it is thought that many architects, surveyors and skilled builders may have been recruited from the provinces and worked under Roman direction. The Romans directed the building of roads, forums with a **basilica**, public baths, temples, theatres and amphitheatres. They also introduced their figurative styles in sculptures, wall paintings, mosaics, jewellery and other crafts. Local craftsmen were taught by the Romans to produce decorations for the Roman houses.

Hadrian's Wall

Hadrian's Wall is probably the best known remaining Roman structure in Britain. It was ordered to be built by Emperor Hadrian to guard the northern frontier of Roman lands. It is 118 kilometres (73 miles) long and was completed in A.D. 136. The walls are 6 metres (20 feet) high and 3 metres (10 feet) thick.

Ceramic pot decorated with large indented "S"s. This pot was made in England some time between the 3rd century B.C. and the Roman Conquest.

Going Places: Transportation, Exploration and Communication

Trade contact between the early Britons and other civilisations were established during in the 5th and 2nd centuries B.C., and increased steadily after about 100 B.C. At this time the principal port was Hengistbury Head in Hampshire, and the Veneti people of Brittany were conducting a regular tin trade from Cornwall. There is little doubt that early traders reached the Colne River in present day Lancashire and carried back slaves. Slave chains from early times have been found at Lords' Bridge, Cambridgeshire.

Roads

There is little evidence of Celtic roads, but because there were trade centres, roads of some kind must have existed. Such tracks would have been kept clear of brambles and weeds, and causeways of layers of trees and brushwood would have been constructed across bogs. Early bridges were made from wood, and boats and ferries were used to cross rivers and straits. It is thought that the Romans may have built over the old Celtic roads and tracks in the same manner as they built over shrines and sacred sites. Forms of transport included chariots, four-wheeled waggons, horses and pack-horses, and foot transport.

The Romans in Britain built approximately 9,000 kilometres (5,580 miles) of roads which linked towns and ports. The roads were used by Roman armies, and by Roman officials collecting taxes and sending messages. Traders used the roads to travel from town to town, and farmers used them to take their produce to the markets.

This ship model found in Derry, Ireland, is thought to represent a ship intended for the high seas. This model was probably used as an offering to the gods.

Waterways

Boats of all sizes travelled up the Thames River and all streams capable of taking boats were used to move grain, vegetables, pottery and other manufactured goods as well as building materials. Caesar noted that the Celtic ships were well-suited to the varied conditions in which they sailed. They were described as being made of oak, with anchors held fast by chains and fitted with sails made of leather.

Unlike the Roman ships, the Celtic ones could sail during high winds and storms, and were not in danger while standing in open seas. It was also noted by the Romans that the Celts were exceptionally good boatsmen.

Music, Dancing and Recreation

The Celts loved music, and instrumental and vocal music were a part of festive gatherings where people were entertained by harpists and players on the timpan, and by bards. Other musical instruments played by the Celts included lyres, pipes, drums and trumpets. There are stories which tell of the magical properties of some music, and of spells cast by some musicians. These stories come from legends which have their origins in old Celtic customs. However, because the songs were not written down, they have been lost.

Although it is presumed that the Celts danced, little is known of the actual dances performed. Celtic figures have been found of dancers and musicians, both men and women, but that is all that survives.

Festivals

The Celtic year was divided into four main parts and each part was preceded by a great religious festival which was accompanied by feasting, games, sport and solemn religious observances. Listed below are some Celtic festivals.

Imbolc	This festival is somewhat obscure, but because it was concerned with lambing, it is thought to have been a pastoral festival.
Beltaine	This was connected with the worship of the ancient Celtic god Belenos. It was a festival connected with fertility to encourage the growth of cattle and crops. It is thought that at this festival the Celts lit bonfires and between these fires the Druids drove the cattle in a symbolic gesture to purify them and protect them from disease. (Beltaine fires were still lit in Scotland until quite recent times.)
Lughnasa	This was a festival to honour the god Lug. Plays and stories were enacted which told of Lug and his victories and achievements. This festival traditionally lasted for a month.
Samain	This was an end of summer festival and marked the beginning of a New Year. A marriage between the tribal god and a nature goddess was celebrated.

Flat bronze spoons made by the Celts in the 1st century A.D. These spoons were probably used for ritual offerings.

Roman Influence

The Romans exerted the most influence on upper class Britons who lived in the Roman towns.

The Romans established their own entertainments and recreations, which included public baths, theatres, amphitheatres and hunting.

The Romans built amphitheatres at Dorchester and Caerleon in Britain where combats between gladiators and animals (usually bears) took place. Romans enjoyed spectacle sports such as fighting events, wrestling, boxing and chariot racing.

Only five Roman theatres are known to have been built in Britain which could mean that this entertainment was not quite so popular.

The Romans built public baths in Britain, and Romans seem to have spent a great deal of time at these establishments. Children, soldiers and slaves were admitted free to the baths, but others usually had to pay to use the baths.

Roman amphitheatre built during the Roman period at Verulamium (St Albans, north of London).

Wars and Battles

In Celtic society, people were often at war with each other. Many Celtic folk heroes were warriors. What we know of Celtic warfare comes from Roman accounts.

Polybius (200–118 B.C.), a Greek historian from Rome, described how the mass of armies drew up with opposing chariots, driving up and down the enemy ranks. Warriors shouted hysterically to intimidate their opponents. The sides of waggons were beaten violently, horns were sounded, and people screamed and bellowed to increase the general uproar. Many warriors painted their bodies and faces with woad (blue vegetable dye) while others displayed the colour red wherever possible. Even horse trappings were highly decorated.

At the second stage of battle warriors would be driven onto the battle field and would alight to deliver personal challenges. Each warrior would alight from his chariot, which would retire to the background and wait to be called forth. It was only after the individual combats had taken place that the general battle would commence.

Cissbury Ring, a Briton hill fort, was used as a place of refuge during the New Stone Age, the Iron Age and the Roman Occupation.

Celtic Battle Dress

This varied considerably with some warriors wearing highly decorative battle dress and others wearing nothing at all. Some Celtic warriors were described as charioteers dressed in a battle tunic of skins covered by a black mantle or cloak, and helmet. Although most warriors went into battle bare headed, helmets were worn by some, most probably by chieftains.

Weapons

Swords were of prime importance in battle. The bronze cut and thrust sword was eventually replaced by the more durable and stronger iron sword. These swords often had hilts of gold and ivory. Swords were carried in scabbards with decorated bronze sheaths. Round or oval wooden shields were used and leather was sometimes used as a protective covering. Long slashing swords and spears are also mentioned as battle weapons.

Hadrian's Wall was built during A.D. 120–128 in northern England from the east coast to the west coast, to keep the Picts and Celts of Scotland out of Roman Britain.

Hill Forts

These were places of permanent or temporary refuge.

In the south-west of Britain at South Cadbury archaeologists have excavated the best example so far discovered of the prehistoric hill forts built by the ancient Britons. The hilltop itself was occupied on occasions from the 3rd millennium B.C. It was abandoned during the Roman period but used again in later times. Inside the fort was a huge rectangular hall which had been divided to provide accommodation in one part.

The Roman Invasions

The Roman forces which invaded Britain in A.D. 43 included four legions and 40,000 additional men. The Roman forces were heavily armoured, well-trained and organised into a system where soldiers could be rapidly supplied and replaced.

In spite of the resistance by the Britons, the Romans, because of their superior fighting forces and numbers, continued to win battles and by A.D. 47, their armies occupied much of Britain. By the year A.D. 90 the main Roman military bases were at York, Chester and Caerleon. Where the Roman armies were victorious over the Britons, many of their defeated soldiers were recruited into the Roman army.

Hadrian's Wall was built in the north across the Solway-Tyne isthmus and this marked the permanent frontier of the Roman empire in Britain. On occasions the tribes from the north succeeded in getting past this wall. Small forts (called milecastles) were built along the wall spaced at intervals of one Roman mile. Other forts were built at lesser intervals.

Inventions and Special Skills

Ogham Alphabet

This script, dating from the 4th century A.D., was used for writing the Irish and Pictish languages on stone monuments. It consisted of strokes and notches comprising an alphabet of 20 letters. The origin of this alphabet has not yet been confirmed. Although more than 500 inscriptions in ogham have been found, most are very short, and are usually only names.

Megaliths and Menhirs

These huge stones (from the Greek *mega* meaning large, and *lithos* meaning stone) were raised into place by ancient people in many parts of Europe and Britain. Megaliths were usually used to mark graves while menhirs, often placed in circles, such as Stonehenge, may have had other uses such as calendrical uses. The reasons for building many of these megalithic monuments is still not completely understood.

Hill Forts

Hill forts, although not a specific feature of Iron Age Britain as some date back to earlier times, were elaborate defence systems characteristic of the Iron Age. These hill forts had multiple ramparts and confusing and complicated entrances to make conquest by attacking armies as difficult as possible. An example of an Iron Age hill fort is Hod Hill in Dorset where a later Roman fort was built within it to make use of the already existing features. Maiden Castle

Bronze handle, in the shape of a human figure, from a short sword. This handle, from the 1st century B.C., was made by the Celts. The Celts were skilled bronze-smiths.

(also in Dorset) is the most famous hill fort in Britain. Little is known about the warriors of the British Stone Age who defended from these hill forts.

Circular Houses

These were typical dwellings of wattle and daub walls and thatched roofs, with clay or turf foundations. Sometimes several of these would be clustered together to form small settlements. As the houses were built of perishable materials none of these have survived. In areas where trees were scarce, circular houses were built of stone. Some of these have survived such as the one at Skara Brae.

Druids

Very little is known about the Druids although they were a very important class in Celtic society. The Romans, including Caesar, wrote of their observations of Druids. The Druids themselves have left very few records of their real power and functions. The Druids are be-lieved to have been a priestly class who were also responsible for teaching and legal affairs. They took charge of public and private sacrifices and other religious rituals.

Caesar remarked that Druidism originated in Britain and that those who wanted to study the subject went there. Although Druidism was suppressed by the Romans in Britain, it continued in Ireland for some time.

Tolerance and Adoption of the Roman Culture

Some scholars believe that even throughout the time of Roman occupation, Britain was more British than Roman. Some Britons adopted the Roman way of doing things but some, especially the highland people, resisted this strongly. Roman technology and knowledge were used on the farms by the Britons, and Roman gods and goddesses were incorporated into the existing religious beliefs and practices. This included bestowing two names (Roman and non-Roman) on gods which were seen as being similar. Roman dress was also adopted by some Britons who also accepted Roman (Latin) education for their sons. Some Latin words were adopted especially if the object was introduced by the Romans and the Britons had no word of their own. However, after the Romans left Britain, many of the Roman ways were discarded.

The remains of some circular stone houses have been found, such as this one at Grimspound, an early Bronze Age village. These ruins show the entrance to the hut.

Why the Civilisation Declined

Eventually the Britons, together with the Saxons (from the un-Romanised world of Germany who had settled in Britain), and the Scots (from Ireland) began to challenge the Romans in Britain. The Picts (from Scotland) had also become troublesome from about A.D. 343. Frontiers of the Roman empire elsewhere, were also being attacked. The Huns from the north of Europe advanced south and captured Rome in A.D. 410, at which time the Roman army and administration withdrew from Britain.

This silver dish, made in the 4th century A.D., was a part of the Mildenhall Silver Treasure.

At the end of the Roman occupation in the 5th century A.D., the Romans buried their tools, coins and other treasures, hoping to re-turn and recover them later when the troubled times were over. This did not happen and some of these hoards such as the **Mildenhall Silver Treasure** have been discovered.

Without the Roman presence, the Roman way of doing things was quickly forgotten. The towns were gradually abandoned and many of the great Roman roads fell into disrepair. Other people such as the Angles, Saxons and Jutes came to Britain after the Romans. The Angles, Saxons and Jutes came to settle and eventually to conquer the lands and alter, yet again, the civilisation of the ancient Britons.

Glossary

Amphitheatre An open-air threatre where gladiatorial games took place. It was surrounded on all sides by tiers of seats built upon banks of earth. In Britain the only amphitheatre carefully studied is one at Caerleon which was hollowed out of a hillside. It is estimated to have held 6,000 people and was probably used for military parades as well as gladiatorial games. Other amphitheatres were at Silchester, Dorset and Caerwent.

Aqueduct An artificial channel for carrying water. In Britain, the best example so far discovered is at Lincoln. It was designed to supply water to dwellers on a hilltop site which would otherwise have needed very deep wells.

Bard A poet in the ancient (and later) Celtic societies. In Celtic they were called Bardi which indicated that they not only sang songs, but also composed them.

Basilica A large Roman oblong building used as a hall of justice and public meeting place.

Brehon Laws (also known as Feinechus) These were ancient laws of Ireland. Although these were not written down until the 7th century A.D. and are difficult to translate, they had their origins in unwritten laws dating back to the Iron Age.

Britons (also called Bretons) The name given to the people inhabiting Britain before the Anglo-Saxon invasions which began in the 5th century A.D.

Celts These people dominated western and central Europe during the last half of the 1st millennium B.C. They were divided into numerous tribes with the Druids as their religious and legal leaders. The Celts arrived in Britain in two waves: the first in about 2000 B.C., and the second in about 200 B.C. The Celts arrived first as a prospecting people who later settled, grew crops and grazed animals. They constructed hill forts to protect their settlements. They were skilled people using iron for everyday tools and weapons and bronze for ornaments. The population of Britain in Roman times was mainly Celtic.

Coligny Calendar This is a fragmentary bronze calendar and is the oldest extensive example of writing in a Celtic language. It measured 150 by 105 centimetres (60 by 42 inches) and was divided into 16 vertical columns providing a table of 62 consecutive lunar months with two intercalary months. Each month was divided into a bright half and a dark half.

Concentric circles Circles having a common centre.

Coulter A sharp blade or wheel attached to the beam of a plough and used to cut the earth.

Cremate To reduce to ashes. This usually refers to reducing a corpse to ashes as opposed to burying it.

Cult A distinct group with its own particular religious rites and ceremonies. Cults usually have a smaller following than a more established religion.

Cup-and-Ring Marks A particular kind of carved mark found in many places throughout Britain. The meaning of these marks is not yet completely understood.

Diocese Bishop's district; area administered by a bishop or other clergyman.

Divination The discovering or foretelling of events by supernatural means. Some methods of divination were quite drastic, for example, during some important occasions a person was stabbed and by observing the way in which the person fell and the movements of various parts of the body, diviners proported to foretell the future. Another ritual of the ancient Britons was called "tarb-fis", which involved the slaughter of a bull and the making of a broth from it. The seer bathed in the broth, ate the meat and then slept. The future was then supposed to appear in a dream.

Domesticate To tame, usually animals or birds, from a wild or natural state, so that they can be controlled by humans.

Druid The learned and priestly class of the ancient Celts. They were responsible for private and public sacrifices, education, laws and justices.

Emmer An early type of wheat.

Flax A plant whose fibre is manufactured into a linen thread and woven into fabrics.

Graffiti Drawings or writing scratched on a wall or other surface. Archaeologists and historians regarded graffiti as the everyday writing and reading matter of people.

Hadrian's Wall One of the largest Roman remains in Britain. It is a wall 118 kilometres (73 miles) long built from Wallsend (Tyne) to Bowness (on the Solway Firth) to keep back the invading northern armies. The thick walls were destroyed three times by northern tribes. Large sections of the wall still exist.

Hemp A tall plant, the fibre of which is used to make coarse fabrics and rope.

Martyr One who would rather be put to death than speak against their religion.

Mead An alcoholic drink made by fermenting honey, water, malt and yeast.

Mildenhall Silver Treasure Roman silver treasure of 34 pieces unearthed in 1942 at Mildenhall. Most of the pieces are 4th century and some originated in Mediterranean factories. The treasure contains a great dish (60 centimetres, or 24 inches in diameter) as well as platters, bowls and smaller pieces. Some pieces have Christian inscriptions.

Mosaics A picture or decoration used in Roman buildings and made of small pieces of stone or glass of different colours inlaid to form a design.

Mystery Plays A Medieval religious drama usually dealing with life, death and the resurrection of Jesus.

Ogham alphabet An alphabet of 20 letters dating from the 4th century A.D. and used for writing the Irish and Pictish languages.

Polar Ice Cap Permanent ice at the north and south poles.

Rampart A broad elevation or mound with a fortification which helped to defend a building or area from oncoming attack.

Shroud A large cloth or sheet used to cover or conceal. A shroud was often placed around a body before burial.

Spelt An early variety of wheat.

Stonehenge A setting of large stones in a circle which is surrounded by earthwork. It was built during the late New Stone Age and finished during the early Bronze Age (1800 to 1400 B.C.), and is located in Wiltshire. The stones are arranged in such a manner so that certain movements of the sun, moon and planets can be observed and measured.

Tundra An area where the vegetation consists of small stunted plants and lichens usually found in cold areas.

Volcanic rock Rocks which have formed in ancient times from the molten lava of a volcano.

Woad A blue paint obtained from the juice of the isatis, a hybrid species. The ancient Britons painted their faces with woad before going into battle, possibly to give themselves a more terrifying appearance. Woad was also used to dye cloth.

The Ancient Britons: Some Famous People and Places

Boudicca, Queen of the Iceni

Boudicca, Queen of the Iceni tribe led a rebellion against the Romans in about A.D. 60–61.

Boudicca's husband, Prasutagus, was King of the Iceni tribe who inhabited south-eastern England. In A.D. 59 Prasutagus died, leaving half his kingdom to the Romans and the other half to his wife, Boudicca, and two daughters.

The Romans went against Prasutagus's wishes and decided the whole kingdom belonged to the Roman Empire. Previously, the Romans had given some of the Briton tribes, including the Iceni, money. After Prasutagus's death, the Romans said that the money was a loan, and they wanted it repaid immediately.

Roman officials and soldiers moved into the Iceni's territory seizing estates from the nobles, and everything the poor owned. Boudicca, who tried to resist, was flogged.

After this, the Britons organised secret meetings: the nobles, peasants and Druids all participated, calling on the Britons to rebel. Boudicca was chosen as their leader.

Once Boudicca organised the forces, they descended on Camulodunum and sacked the whole town including the Roman temple. The Britons then sacked Londinium and Verulamium.

The Romans eventually organised two armies who moved in on the Britons, and savagely murdered them. After this defeat Boudicca poisoned herself, and the Britons mourned her deeply.

Julius Caesar

The Roman Julius Caesar lived from about 102 to 44 B.C. and carried out raids on Britain. The first raid was in 55 B.C. but was not very successful. In 54 B.C. Caesar returned with a large force of 25,000 legionnaires and 2,000 cavalry. Caesar realised that the Britons were a very strong and powerful enemy. He also feared that there would be rebellions in Roman Gaul so instead of attempting to conquer the Britons, he made a treaty with them and withdrew, making Britain part of the Roman world.

St Patrick and St Alban

St Patrick was born in Britain in about A.D. 373. He has been credited with bringing Christianity to Ireland. He was the last missionary of the British church before the Anglo-Saxon invasions. St Patrick wrote two short works, the *Convessio* (*Confession*) which was an autobiography, and the *Epistole* (*Letters*) which he wrote in later life and is an account of the ill-treatment received by some Christian captives at the hands of the British chieftain, Coroticus.

By the 7th century A.D. there were many legends about St Patrick. One legend says that he drove all the snakes out of Ireland into the sea, and that he used the shamrock (a three-leaved plant) to explain the Holy Trinity (three persons in one god) to people. The shamrock has come to be the national symbol of Ireland.

St Alban was the earliest known British Christian martyr who was executed in about A.D. 208 or 209 outside Verulamium. By A.D. 400, this place had become St Alban's Shrine where eventually the largest English Benedictine Abbey and the town of St Albans was founded.

Cassivellaunus

Cassivellaunus was a powerful British chieftain who lived in the first century B.C. His tribe was the Catuvellauni, a Belgiac people who lived where modern Hertfordshire now stands. He led his people against the Romans and made good use of guerilla tactics and chariots. He was finally defeated when the Romans, under Julius Caesar, captured their main fort (where present day Wheathampstead now stands). Cassivellaunus was made to provide hostages and to pay tribute each year to Rome.

Queen Cartimandua and Venutius

Cartimandua lived during the first century A.D. and was Queen of the Brigantes, a tribe in northern Britain. Early in the Roman conquest of Britain, Cartimandua signed a treaty with Rome. Many of her subjects disapproved of this and rebelled. In A.D. 48 the Roman forces helped her put down these uprisings. The British leader Caratacus was captured by Cartimandua's forces three years later and Caratacus was handed over to the Romans.

In A.D. 57, her husband Venutius tried to gain the support of the anti-Roman subjects and overthrow her so he could rule in his own right. Again the Roman forces came to her assistance. A reconciliation followed between her and Venutius and they ruled together until A.D. 69, after which time she left her husband. Venutius tried to organise an uprising and over-throw her again, and yet again the Roman forces supported Cartimandua. After this time nothing further is known about Cartimandua. Venutius was leader of the Brigantes in A.D. 71 when they were defeated by the Romans.

The Saxon Shore

This was a system of nine forts stretching from present day Brancaster in Norfolk to Portchester. It was established in about A.D. 275. They were built to defend south-east Roman Britain from the Anglo-Saxon raiders. Each fort protected a harbour and housed troops who were to defend the shore against any landings. In A.D. 343 the army was upgraded and made more mobile and the office of Count of the Saxon Shore came into being.

Portchester is the best known of the Saxon Shore forts. It covers about 4 hectares (9 acres).

Silchester

Silchester, south-west of Reading, contains the site of the important Roman town of Calleva Attrebatum which was an important centre for the Roman road system. Celtic earthworks, a forum and basilica, an inn, baths, temples and a Christian church and ampitheatre have all been located there. It was planned on sym-metrical lines and was rebuilt in its Roman form during the first and early second centuries A.D. The city was excavated by the Society of Antiquaries.

Sextus Julius Frontinus

Julius Frontinus was a governor of Roman Britain from A.D. 74 to 78. He achieved the conquest of Wales except for the conquest of Anglesey which was achieved by Agricola. Following this he established fortresses at Caerleon and Chester.

Stonehenge

This is probably the best known prehistoric monument in Britain dating back to about 2300 B.C. when work on it is thought to have begun. Two further stages of construction took place. About 2000 to 1700 B.C. the circles of bluestones were constructed. These were brought from the Prescelly Mountains in Dyfed. The final stage of Stonehenge is thought to have been added in about 1700 to 1500 B.C. This included the raising of the circle of thirty huge sarsen stones which were joined by lintels plus the horseshoe of larger sarsen stones and a concentric circle and horseshoe of bluestones.

Index

Acknowledgements

The author and publishers are grateful to the following for permission to reproduce copyright photographs and prints:

Australasian Nature Transparencies: (Silvestris) pp.11, 24, (NHPA) p.12, (Pavel German) p.13; Ronald Sheridan/The Ancient Art and Architecture Collection pp.9, 14, 16, 19 bottom, 20, 25, 28, 29, 36, 37, 38, 40, 41; Werner Forman Archive cover, 15, 17, 18, 19 top, 21, 22, 23, 27, 30, 31, 32, 33, 34, 35, 39.

While every care has been taken to trace and acknowledge copyright, the publishers tender their apologies for any accidental infringement where copyright has proved untraceable. They would be pleased to come to a suitable arrangement with the rightful owner in each case.

Cover design, maps and art: Stephen Pascoe

First published 1989 by
THE MACMILLAN COMPANY OF AUSTRALIA PTY LTD
107 Moray Street, South Melbourne 3205
6 Clarke Street, Crows Nest 2065

Associated companies and representatives throughout the world.

National Library of Australia cataloguing in publication data.

Odijk, Pamela, 1942–
  The ancient Britons.

  Includes index.
  ISBN 0 333 47776 6.

  1. Great Britain — History — To 55 B.C. — Juvenile literature. I. Title. (Series: Odijk, Pamela, 1942–   Ancient world).

936.1'01

Set in Optima by Setrite Typesetters, Hong Kong
Printed in Hong Kong

Oceania | Europe | Africa

c50 000 B.C. Aborigines inhabit continent

40 000 Evolution of man

Time scale (left axis): 8000, 7500, 7000, 6500, 6000, 5500, 5000, 4500, 4000, 3500, 3000, 2500, 2000, 1500, 1000, 500, B.C./A.D. 0, 500, 1000, 1500, 2000

Oceania

Australian Aborigines
- Torres and Bass Straits under water
- Lake Nitchie settled
- South Australian settlements
- Ord Valley settlement
- Dutch explorers sight Aborigines
- First White settlers

Maori
- Legend: Kupe found New Zealand and told people how to reach there
- Maori arrive
- Great Britain annexed New Zealand

Melanesians
- Europeans dominate
- Cook's voyages
- Christianity is introduced

Europe

Greeks
- Neolithic Age
- Settled agriculture
- Bronze Age
- Crete — palaces
- Mainland building
- Dark Age
- Colonisation
- City-states established
- Classical Age
- Wars — lands extended
- Hellenistic Age
- Empire divided, lands lost. Culture enters new phase

Romans
- Rome found
- Republic established
- Rome expands through Italy and foreign lands
- Empire begins: Augustus — emperor
- End of Western Roman Empire

Angles, Saxons & Jutes
- Hengist and Horsa arrived in Kent
- England: 12 kingdoms
- Athelstan rules all England
- Norman Conquest

Britons
- Hunting and gathering
- Megalithic monuments raised
- Farms and buildings established
- Ogham alphabet in use
- Roman invasion
- Britain becomes two provinces
- Saxons settle

Vikings
- The Baltic — freshwater lake
- The first farmers
- Bronze Age
- Celtic Iron Age
- Roman Iron Age
- Vendel period
- Army invade England
- Christianity adopted
- Viking laws recorded

Africa

Egyptians
- Egypt-early farms
- Predynastic
- Old Kingdom
- Giza pyramids
- Middle Kingdom
- New Kingdom
- New Kingdom declines
- Persian conquest
- Greek conquest
- Roman rule

First Africans
- 40 000 Evolution of man
- Farm settlements
- Increased trade across Sahara
- Sahara becomes desert
- Kushites
- Nok
- Greek influence
- Kushites' power ends
- Arabs settle east coast
- Christian European slave trade
- Europeans divide Africa